WAVES OF YOU

LOVE POEMS

Copyright © 2021 by Michelle G. Stradford.

All rights reserved. No part of this book may be used or reproduced in any manner without written permission from the author except for use in reviews or articles.

ISBN 9781735399850
ISBN 9781735399843 (eBook)

Edited by Eva Xan

This book is a work of fiction. The names, characters, places, and events are the product of the author's imagination or used factiously. Any resemblance to actual events or locales or persons, living or deceased, is coincidental.

Sunurchin, LLC

WAVES OF YOU

LOVE POEMS

Michelle G. Stradford

Also, By Michelle G. Stradford

Rise Unstoppable

I'm Rising: Determined. Confident. Powerful.

When Love Rises

Dear Reader

"Waves of You" is a collection of heartfelt poetry and prose celebrating the magic of romantic love. As I poured my thoughts and experiences onto these pages, I reflected on how love is fragile yet holds tremendous power to bring hearts together despite distance, time, complexities, and differences.

The theme focuses on the joys of love instead of the inevitable heartbreak experienced while navigating through life searching for our soulmates. A follow-up collection is underway addressing heartbreak and healing, so please stay tuned.

I grew up near Myrtle Beach, frolicking in the waves with my family and friends. I walked on the ocean shore hand in hand with my first boyfriend and later with my dear husband and children picking up seashells, reveling in the swirl of water kissing our feet. The ocean has always had a powerful pull on me. Its beauty and symbology, the waves' rush and ebbing, have been metaphors for my romance with life for as long as I can remember. Thus, this book's title and the theme of the chapters revolve around the fluidity of love flowing in waves.

Romantic relationships are nuanced with layers of meaning and often charged with emotions that we struggle to understand. We all experience love differently and search for our unique ways to express what others mean to us. I hope you will find meaning in these pages and feel inspired to find your own love language.

DEDICATION

I dedicate this book to my amazing sisters and brothers who inspire and uplift me constantly. Your unconditional love and support extend beyond the DNA we share. I love you each endlessly.

TABLE OF CONTENTS

WAVES 1
    Finding You 2
    Beautiful Words 3
    Mystic Universes 4
    The Light 5
    Sedated 6
    Open Path 7
    Flourish Together 8
    Joyful Notes 9
    Constancy 10
    Falter 11
    No Secret 12
    Exacting Perfection 13
    Complete Love 14
    Thank You Gravity 15
    Winning 16
    Misperceptions 17
    Overtaken 18
    Never Stopped 19
    Pearls 20
    Powerful Light 21
    Fulfillment 22
    Soul Search 23
    Stalked 24
    Exuberance 25
    Growing a Love 26
    Transparent 27
    Kernels for My Soul 28
    Indescribable 29
    Below My Surface 30
    Discovering You 31
    Catch Hold 32
    Your Pulse 33
    Passive Love 34
    Ripples 35
    Deep Ties 36
    Intuitive 37
    Thirst for More 38
    Lights On 39
    Found Home 40
    Captivating 41
    Broken Melodies 42

Love Blooms	43
Found Treasure	44
Extravagant	45
Taming Love	46
Authenticity	47
Poetic Tapestry	48
My Future	49
Destined	50
Hidden	51
You Sustain Me	52
Eyes on Me	53
Hint of Charm	54
Seize the Love	55
Renewed	56
Love Unfiltered	57
Beyond Sweet	58
Pillar	59
Intrigued	60
Affliction	61
Past Behind	62
Love Language	63
Reclaimed Me	64
Love Religion	65
Unwavering Faith	66
Molten Fate	67

CURRENTS	69
Artwork	70
Balmy Summers	71
My King	72
Ebb Your Flow	73
Old Thirst	74
Silent Guide	75
Heartbeat	76
To the Flame	77
The Wilderness	78
Seared	79
Low Tides	80
Low Burn	81
Canvas	82
The Getaway	83
Fingerprints	84
French Seduction	85
Our Formula	86
You Linger	87
Match My Fire	88

- **Drum My Beat** ... 89
- Simmer ... 90
- **Ocean of Songs** ... 91
- **Unteachable** ... 92
- Wild Currents ... 93
- First Light ... 94
- Undone ... 95
- Powerful Sage ... 96
- Sun-Kissed ... 97
- See Level ... 98
- Urgency of Love ... 99
- **Cascades** ... 100
- Heights Untold ... 101
- Fever ... 102
- Prerequisites ... 103
- **Your Nectar** ... 104
- **Reverberate** ... 105
- Edge of Breathless ... 106
- You Free Me ... 107
- Confession ... 108
- Enchanted ... 109
- Moved ... 110
- My Mystic Love ... 111
- **Entangled** ... 112
- Dangerous Tides ... 113
- Shared Home ... 114
- Sanguine Summer ... 116
- Heated Lies ... 117
- By the Sea ... 118
- Basking ... 119
- Borrowed Lies ... 120
- The Fire ... 121

IMMERSED ... 123
- Magic Life ... 124
- Held ... 125
- Imperfect Love ... 126
- **Reticence** ... 127
- Lines Drawn ... 128
- Perpetual ... 129
- Blissful ... 130
- Fortress ... 131
- Epic Beginning ... 132
- Same You ... 133
- Changed Me ... 134
- Top Priority ... 135

You Break Me Free	137
Warmed Hearts	138
Virtuous	140
Lasting Allure	141
Stoic Grace	142
Advancing	143
Nostalgic Trips	144
Naked Words	145
Love Reaches	146
Stronger Us	147
Heartstrings	148
Our Anniversary	149
Immortal Love	150
My Cover	151
Horizons	152
Lift You	153
Bloom in Silence	154
Unwavering Faith	155
What I Want	156
Commitment	157
Rivers Raging	158
Our Happily Ever After	159
Love Knows	160
Raw Truth	161
Light Beams	162
Year to Renew	163
Eternal Flame	164
Futures Spring	165
The Sunlight	166
Waves of You	167

FROM THE AUTHOR	169
ACKNOWLEDGMENTS	171
ABOUT THE AUTHOR	173
OTHER BOOKS	175

*My ocean is
brimming
with poetic symmetry.
Each time
you swim nearby,
your waves
overtake me.*

*I am nearly capsized
by the turbulence
of your wake.
As I resurface,
I am newly baptized,
made a believer
in your power
to unbalance me.*

Your Wake

WAVES

*Your heart
is made
of rising sun.
No amount
of darkness can
keep your light
from shining through
or me from
finding you.*

Finding You

When you said,
"holding my hand
in silence while
I was breaking
turned the lock
that reopened my heart,
releasing pain that long
held me a prisoner,"
my tears spilled over,
as those words
held more beauty
than anything ever
gifted to me before.

Beautiful Words

You read my chapters
one by one, smiling
and delighting in each story,
memorizing my lines,
then finally grasping
that the long path
I have walked forms
the genesis of my fears.

Your fingers traced
the rivulets of my tears
as you paged through
my list of high hopes,
and ill-fitting dreams.

Then you kissed
my eyelids
and whispered,
"You are far more
than a page-turning
intrigue; you're a series
of mystic universes
yet to be explored."

Mystic Universes

*I can never replace
all that you have lost,
but I will fill in the gaps
and help you find
your missing parts.*

*I will transform
into whatever
your heart requires,
become the light
in your dimmest hour.*

The Light

**Why does the power
of your embrace
when you hold me,
so completely
mend the pain
of the deep cuts
I have sustained
from the loves
that hurt before you?
Your arms are healing.
You sedate me.**

Sedated

*I will always leave
a place in my mind
unoccupied for you,
an unlocked entryway,
granting an open path
into my life__
So, you never lose
your way to finding
refuge inside my heart.*

Open Path

You made me believe
that I had prudently
tucked away
a fertile place where love
had not grown,
because the perfect one
had not yet come along.

I rose this morning
to find my heart
planted in our wild
and flourishing garden,
celebrating
the fruits of the seeds
we had sown together.

Flourish Together

When your eyes
alit upon mine,
the joyful notes
that once reigned
over my heart
suddenly began playing
sweet melodies again.

Joyful Notes

**Endless nights
have vanished
into uncertainty
and countless chances
have been lost
to my indecision.**

**Nonetheless,
I will not lose
one further moment
without making you see
how deeply you
have touched me.**

**It is clear that you
have become
my everything.
You are my clarity,
bolstering me
with constancy.**

Constancy

**Of course
I can survive.
Yes, I will go on
without you.**

**The truth is
that
I falter,
and my
heart
palpitates
at the thought
of ever having
to leave you
on the other side
of the gate.**

Falter

*Falling in love
cannot keep secrets.
It whispers messages,
telegraphs delights,
and leaves vestiges
along the way.
It rarely surprises
or sneaks up on you.*

No Secret

You coaxed
my heart open,
peeled away
my armor
and made me see
that every flamboyant
layer of me,
each innate flaw
and beautiful part
was formed in
exacting perfection.

You made me see
and feel that
my rawness
is exceptional,
simply beautiful.

Exacting Perfection

*I felt complete love
the day I swam
through the riptides
of your vulnerabilities
and finally kissed
your shore.*

Complete Love

**Both gravity
and my
sheer will
are the only
abounding forces
that can hold
my heart down
and keep it
from expanding,
then rising
and exploding
like helium balloons
each time your smile
enters a room.**

Thank You Gravity

*You had made a sport
out of losing at love
until I rigged the game
and let you win my heart.
Losing to you has been
the greatest gain of my life.*

Winning

What we first
perceived
to be
wild weeds,
grew into
our burgeoning
love-filled prairie
of blue asters
and yellow poppies.

Misperceptions

I left my gates
unlocked, unguarded
and I was devoid of fear.

I sowed my hopes
in faith, believing
there would be
enough room
in this garden for both
you and me
to grow side by side,
and share
in life's bounties.

I did not expect
to be nurtured
and strengthened
in your care,
nor to grow a love
so astonishing and rare
that it overtook us.

Overtaken

*I always knew
that our love
was destined to be
my truth,
because never
have I ever
stopped falling
for you.*

Never Stopped

*There were portions
of me
that I still believed
were unreachable
and the least worthy
of love
until you revealed
that every part
you had seen
was urgently vital
and invaluable,
just waiting
to fully evolve
into pearls.*

Pearls

Waves of You

Though I had tried
to dim my blinding
bright star
and shuttered out
all that felt right,
because feeling inadequate
made me weep,
you refused to give up
on reaching me.

You coaxed me
out of my shadows
and taught me
not to stand in fear
of the power
of my own light.

Powerful Light

Michelle G. Stradford

I had always
felt a hollowness,
an urgent
transparency
until I poured
everything,
all of me
into us.
Then I could not
stop the waves
of feelings
from overflowing
into oceans
of fulfillment.

Fulfillment

Waves of You

*Your love does not
take my breath away.
It breathes life into me,
no matter how high
you lift my soul
or how deep
you send me
searching.*

Soul Search

I woke up smiling
and suddenly in love.

Then, I remembered
all those stolen glances
while you were speaking.

I discovered the lost words
that I could never find
when we were talking.

The subtle images of you
dancing behind my dreams
while I was sleeping
have come to life.

Love is a silent stalker.

Stalked

*I have yet to discover
a bottom or an end
to the boundless joy
making my heart sing
and exuberance for life
simply being
in your presence
brings.*

Exuberance

We planted a seed
that germinated slowly
through lively conversations.
It grew a little each day
between a subtle touch
and thoughtful gesture.

Unseen,
it slipped silently
beneath each
softly spoken word.
One day, we awoke to find
we had not fallen,
but had grown in love.

Growing a Love

*Though your words
are still wallowing
in self-convicted
denial,
your eyes have seen
way past
mere possibilities
to commitment.*

*Your heart
is a two-way mirror.
I see you
searching
for me...*

Transparent

Michelle G. Stradford

My soul was starved
of hope and trust.
I had given up on passion
and stopped believing
I would ever belong
to an "us"
until you lifted me up,
kicked away the past
and taught me how to subsist
on small kernels of hope,
and to store them up
to build a love that lasts.

Kernels for My Soul

You are a work of art:
indescribable
and a sight
to be experienced,
making it impossible
to read you
or capture your essence
in mere words.

Indescribable

Michelle G. Stradford

You acted
on your courage,
deep diving
below my surface,
determined to explore
the wildest dreams
my mind could hold.

Then, you searched
for the colorful
secret treasures,
lining the rainforests
of my soul.

Below My Surface

Waves of You

I loved you
prior to heeding
the loud insistence
to search far and wide
and long before
I could know
of your existence.

Life set me on
a winding journey
of learning
its tough lessons
so that I could discern
your true essence
and fully treasure you
in our first moment
of discovery.

Discovering You

*Instinctively, I knew
exactly how to hold you.
Years before, my arms
were taught
how to catch
your bouncing heart,
cradle and enfold you
close to my chest
and never let go.*

Catch Hold

**The feel
of the insistent
strumming
of your pulse
is my ear music.
It keeps me humming,
never leaving me
alone.
I carry your heartbeat
with me
wherever I roam.**

Your Pulse

I love you from afar,
watering the roots
of our linkage
with my bashful hands.

I drop interesting
hints about us,
while averting my
telling eyes.

Yet, I hope our casual
acquaintance will grow
into an affection
without me ever
revealing
my true intention.

Passive Love

Waves of You

I hear your words,
the tough talk
and the denial
in your voice.
But your eyes
reveal the rising
fervor for me
that ripples
like truth serum
through your mind.

Ripples

*Yes, I can exist without
the care of your attention,
but I will not thrive
without our deep
and philosophical
discussions,
or the hope you inspire
through our soulful
connection.*

Deep Ties

You quickly discovered
my reservoir of spirituality
that no one else
knew existed
and assumed
it was deep enough
to hold you
and wide enough
to live in.
Your heart
is intuitive.

Intuitive

Michelle G. Stradford

Your passion for life
relit my aching thirst
for more:
an authentic experience.

In you, my search
has been revived.
Your heart senses
in multiple dimensions.

You possess a magical mind
that spins time,
and dwells in the realm
beyond all known
possibilities.

Yes, this yearning
might well be quenched
by the taste of enchantment
on your lips
and the intoxicating feelings
like liqueur
pouring between us.

Thirst for More

Waves of You

I invited you
in for a virtual tour
of my heart.
You turned the light on
and played poignant
French love songs
on my piano,
then promptly
made me your home.

Lights On

*I was in search
of a secret refuge,
a temporary respite.*

*Instead, I discovered
that I felt at home
inside of your heart,
a permanent place
I'd already made my own.*

So, I never turned back.

Found Home

If I must share you,
please do not allow
the world to see
your captivating smile.

All the Lost Souls
will line our streets
for miles
to find their way
into your heart.

Captivating

Michelle G. Stradford

Your damaged and torn
heart is more beautiful
to me than a shiny new one
still intact that has never
dared to sing
or risked anything;
nor could
scarcely understand
the melancholic lyrics
sung by a blues band.

    Though your past
    goes unspoken,
    you hum the melodies
    of the broken.

    So, I know you will take
    special care of this
kindred soul, singing
but still nursing
my share
of old heartbreaks.

Broken Melodies

Love begins
as a tiny seed,
then grows slowly
into deeds
that whisper meaning
into every word
planting messages
bursting to be heard.
We listen to our hearts
in full bloom.

Love Blooms

You compel me
to share what should
rarely be spoken.

Cautiously, you uncovered
a part of me
that I have
always kept hidden,
leaving me vulnerable
and feeling left open.

Even though I am
still unfinished
and a bit edgy,
you make me shine
like a found treasure.

Found Treasure

*The urgency of wanting
a love that keeps me high
and makes me feel
extravagant
is not too much
to hope for in a world
where they only
minted one you.*

Extravagant

I believed that
acknowledging love
would cause it to wilt
and darken
like a red cut rose.

We plucked
a budding knowing
out of the wild,
then watered
and nurtured it carefully,
refusing to allow
love to die
in our captivity.

Taming Love

*You drew me out
into the stark light,
refusing to allow me
to cower in the shadows
behind my fragile ego,
or let my insecurities
keep chanting no.*

*You would not let me
prevent you from
seeing and experiencing
the authentic person
you have come to love.*

Authenticity

Michelle G. Stradford

I inked my feelings
between the lines
in a hidden poem,
then stitched it into
a permanent tapestry
filled with memories
I dreamed we would
someday make.

My poetry holds
subliminal powers
to summon
the immense emotions
we have never
been able to contain.

I gift it to you.

Poetic Tapestry

Until this moment,
you did not exist.

But in an instant,
I know that without you,
a bleak future
certainly awaits me.

My Future

Michelle G. Stradford

Please respect
that I have embarked
upon a journey
of discovering
the wonders and depths
of personal love.

I hope you will wait
to be invited to join me,
after I have deemed
whether you
are meant to be
a part of my destiny.

Destined

*It is revealing
that I worked
unknowingly
to conceal, discard
the one thing in me
that you needed most.*

*I am grateful that
you discovered
my hidden treasure
before it was
completely buried.*

Hidden

It is ironic that
I have built a life
of self-sufficiency,
educating myself
and gaining all I need
to be comfortable.

I excelled and achieved
each conceived goal
all, so I would never
have to rely on anyone.

Yet here I am,
standing at your door
in search of the epic love
I need to sustain myself.
You possess the one thing
I have never attained
on my own;
to belong with someone.

You Sustain Me

Do not conflate
my silence
with lack of intention.

My gestures and eye language
whisper feelings
I cannot yet mention.

You should have
heard clearly
had you been
paying full attention.

Eyes on Me

Though no one else
may notice,
I catch the tawny lights
dancing in your iris
and the shimmer
of the setting sun
mixed with a smirk
of accomplishment.

That's the endearing
look you get
when you feel
most confident
that you have won
me over with
engineered logic
and a hint of charm.

Hint of Charm

*Losing at love
more times than
I can remember,
fortunately
did not render
me cynical.*

*It made me grateful
that I recognized
yours as an open,
genuine heart
and seized the love
finally intended for me.*

Seize the Love

You peeked in
through my cracks,
coaxed my heart
back open
and showed me
how completely
my scars
had already healed.

You helped me see
that I was renewed,
and my fate
was never sealed
in the pain-filled perpetuity
I had once believed.

Renewed

We discovered
that honoring
and embracing
the unfiltered versions
of ourselves
elevated our love
far higher,
pushing us beyond
all previous experiences
and past relations.

Love Unfiltered

Michelle G. Stradford

I derive great pride
in being
a fully grown,
self-sufficient woman,
fueled by
self-empowerment
and never in need
of anything
or anyone else
to complete me.

Then, you entered
my space,
setting out
to demonstrate
that becoming a WE
and building a life
with you
would not make me
weak or dependent,
but would expand
and sweeten life
far beyond
my imagination.

Beyond Sweet

The unshakeable
foundation
for all love,
earthly, eternal,
and spiritual,
was built upon
the reliable
pillar of self-love.

Pillar

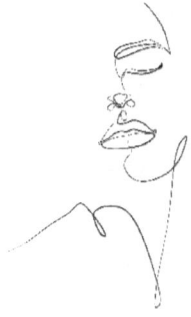

In your unguarded
moment,
I slipped through
a tiny tear
and caught a rare
sight of you
in the place you go to hide
to ruminate and create.

On this softer side,
I stumbled upon
unexpected enchantments,
and uncovered
your new mysteries.

Now I am caught up
in your intrigue,
forever entranced
and trapped inside
of a place in you
I never knew existed.

Intrigued

Why am I afflicted
with ascribing
so much meaning to us,
and feeling so deeply
for you this soon?

I have started to believe
far too completely
in things I cannot see.
Yet, I am incapable
of ending
this addiction to you.

I move towards your light
in blinding trust,
all the while knowing
the speed of this heat
may consume us.

Affliction

Michelle G. Stradford

I am putting the past
behind me,
so, I have forgotten
my yesterdays.

All the weeks,
months and years
that came before are gone,
because you
were not there.
Nothing exists for me
that we did not share.

The me that was
before you
never happened
if it did not include you.
Life commenced
the moment we met.
I just knew.

Your love has made
me new.

Past Behind

*I hold our playful
and messy
love language
in high esteem,
miles above
the serious discussions
steeped in
polite perfection.*

Love Language

Despite how long
I have submerged
vintage feelings for you,
memories of our epic
and unforgettable love
have resurfaced.

They roared in
and crashed ashore
to reclaim me.

Old sensations of you
rise high, overflow
and are too disruptive
to be ignored.

Reclaimed Me

Waves of You

I do not know
precisely when you
became my everything.
Nonetheless, you are
deeply embedded
and so completely
ingrained
in my world
that you
fuel my existence.

You are the reason
that I breathe
and have become
the embodiment
of the religion
I swore to never
believe in.

Love Religion

I held on fast
to my unwavering faith
that, what was
meant to be,
would someday
lead to the one
in search of me.

Just as I was
becoming restless,
fate materialized
and made me
instantly realize
that you are
the manifestation
of these long-awaited
years of unanswered
prayers.

Unwavering Faith

I carried this secret
desire for years,
a one-direction current
circling through me
with nowhere to go.

You finally sensed
my surging energy
responding with
positivity.

When the current
flowed between us,
we exploded into
golden fields
melding together
in a molten fate.

Molten Fate

Michelle G. Stradford

CURRENTS

Michelle G. Stradford

*If you truly
wish to own
my heart,
make
understanding
both my mind and body
your art.*

Artwork

Waves of You

You stir me
like
an unexpected
breeze,
teasing the hair
on my arms
while we're trying
to find
cool relief
from
the balmy summer.

I feel
the temperature
rising
as we converse
with ease,
but
an unspoken
potency
hanging on
to the
humid air
threatens
to overheat us.

Balmy Summers

*One lingering kiss
and I am lost
in your midst.
I swallow all the words
my heart has been
screaming to sing.
Our butterflies flutter,
encircling us in love rings.
From this moment
I crown you king
over my heart.*

My King

Waves of You

Your ripples
roll over and flow
right through me.

A pure love
should not be
this fluid.

Please cease
the ebbing
and stay ashore
to frolic with me.

Ebb Your Flow

Michelle G. Stradford

I felt an old thirst rising
the moment my eyes
found yours again.

You are a dry emptiness
that can never
be quenched.

My glass of you
will never stay filled.

Old Thirst

Waves of You

You move me silently
in undetectable motion
like the moon
leads the sea
in high tide,
calmly coaxing
and directing me
to rise.

You lift me
to zeniths
I never thought
were possible to reach.

Silent Guide

*We continue
this dance
to each other's
heartbeats
long after the music
has ended.*

*I move
to your rhythm
even in my sleep.*

Heartbeat

**I am the moth
so completely enthralled
and drawn to you,
that I would light
my wings on fire
so, we can
burn as two.**

To the Flame

Enticed by
the unexplored
wilderness
lurking beneath
our skin.

We ventured in,
oblivious
to the dangers,
unaware that
our coupling
would unleash
a force too powerful
and unwieldy.

We have lost
all control…

The Wilderness

Waves of You

I feel the heat
in your eyes
searing my skin
from across the room.

Please turn down
your gaze
before I ignite
and I'm set ablaze.

Seared

You are
the only one
who has ever learned
how to rise
and flow
with me
and not dissipate
in the low tides.

Low Tides

This low-burning
hunger cannot
be turned down
after reaching
the melting point.

Once stirred, the heat
will rise and boil over,
transforming us.

Our bond will
forever change.
Love will crystalize,
making us unbreakable
and invincible.

Low Burn

*Your fingers move
over my skin,
seductively
painting abstract images
in bold, commanding colors
until you own
every inch of me.*

I am your canvas.

Canvas

Waves of You

It is difficult to explain
how the sound of your
soothing voice transports
me to places
we have never been.

You utter a word
that suddenly sends
us on a reverie
of exploration
to a getaway for two.

We are locked away
in a French chalet
on a snowy afternoon,
lit with a low fire
slowly inching
the temperature higher.

The Getaway

*This muted passion
for you washes over me
in pastel watercolors
with an urgency
you may not always see,
but I constantly feel.*

*You color my life
with an insistency
that is breathtaking,
leaving your
permanent fingerprints
on my psyche.*

Fingerprints

Waves of You

Your kisses linger
lazily in the room.
My words and worries
melt into possibilities.

I swallow the taste
of Paris,
where my
tensions are teased
into a frenzy,
then
soothed by French wine
and a bittersweet truffle.

My composure slips
as your intense gaze
shifts my footing,
loosening my grasp
on resisting you.

French Seduction

*Every single encounter
with you trembles me
in delight.
Each casual touch,
leaves me imagining
how to replicate
our formula or remix
this chemistry
into an even more
explosive reaction.*

Our Formula

That lingering kiss,
the way you traced
my lower lip
triggered
the start
of a
longing.

It persisted,
leaving me
wanting more,
hours and weeks
before
you walked
out the door.

You Linger

Not only did you
set a spark to the kindling,
you matched
the height of my fire
and unleashed
an awakening.

As I watch us rise higher
and burn brighter,
I wonder how
we can channel
this desire without
getting burned.

Match My Fire

*My heart gave up
every beat
for you
until you
had fallen
into its rhythm,
finally drumming
only for me.*

Drum My Beat

Michelle G. Stradford

Long after I am gone,
you will feel me
still simmering on low,
harboring my goodness
in the soft parts
of your bones,
keeping you warm
until my return.

Simmer

Waves of You

I am an ocean
of songs
serenading
and beckoning you
to wade in.

Come swim with me.

I long to hear your heart
singing in time
as we sway
to each other's motion.

Ocean of Songs

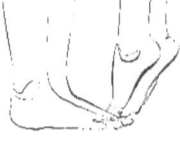

Michelle G. Stradford

I require a love
that is spontaneously
uncontrollable,
bursting on impulse
and rejects any
all-consuming
sense of obligation
to prove something.

There is no substitute
for raw passion,
that deeply spiritual
and unteachable love.
I will acquiesce
to nothing less.

Unteachable

Waves of You

*Uncertain of whether
you felt me too,
I dropped all pretenses,
and took a dive
into your deep end__
ill-prepared, defenseless,
not knowing how to swim
in your erratic currents.
You rode the waves
with me
surfacing in time
to saved me.*

Wild Currents

Michelle G. Stradford

I always want
to be
the first light
you see
when day dawns
over the rolling
turquoise sea.

My heart
will never
set sail again
without you
next to me.

First Light

Waves of You

Your urgency
and sheer honesty
both frighten
and intoxicate me.

I am exhilarated
by your passion
for life,
for me and us.

Being swept up
into your energy
is my dream
come true.
But all this raw
vulnerability
is altering my view.

As strong as I am,
I will come
completely
undone
should I ever face
a day living
without you.

Undone

*Feeling your warm
arms encircling me
is like a powerful sage
infusing my entire body
with a calming,
all-knowing energy.*

Powerful Sage

The sweet dawn
rushes in swiftly
to save me
from a nightmare,
where I wrestled
with
losing you
to the darkest folds
of a restless night.

Then, I awoke
safe in your arms
in the early morn,
warmed by
the golden kiss
of the sun.

Sun-Kissed

You rushed in
on the highest tide,
elevating my pulse
above unsafe
see levels,
overcoming me
with insatiable desire.

See Level

I will never hold back
the urgency
of our powerful love,
because the promise
of tomorrows
may never come.

Be prepared
as I unleash
all of me
and my passion
for you
in unbridled energy.

Urgency of Love
.

Michelle G. Stradford

*Today, your presence
transformed
one ordinary minute
into an unending cascade
of exquisite moments,
filling up what
just yesterday
were endless hours
of my empty existence.*

Cascades

Waves of You

Those intense eyes
locked me tight
in a gripping hold,
refusing to let go.

Your vibe
is unyielding,
surrounding,
then unfolding.

It is leading me
to a place where
uncorked desire awaits,
fizzing and ready
to explode,
lifting us
to heights untold.

Heights Untold

Barely a day
has passed since
our chance meeting
and I have already
caught your fever.

I was too naïve to see
how infectious
and alluring
this tantalizing
attraction could be.

Fever

Your skin on my skin
sends currents
of startling slivers
through me.
This intimacy
is sending signals
that I am not
ready to process.

My mind requires
a cerebral connection
before my body
can respond with affection,
or the walls of my heart
can be breached.

Prerequisites

Michelle G. Stradford

*Upon plucking
the white roses
from your thorny branches
and tasting the nectar
in your kisses,
I discovered what my life
was missing
and knew the fight
for love this earthly
and pure
was more than worth it.*

Your Nectar

Waves of You

Rumbling waves
reverberate through me,
pulsing from a thousand
worlds away.

Your love surrounds,
then surges in me
soothing my aches
and collapsing all past pain,
beneath your
resounding quake.

Reverberate

Michelle G. Stradford

Your kisses lead me
to the top peak
of Sierra Nevada,
then swiftly deep dive
to the Pacific floor,
spinning me into
an effusive wide-eyed
wonderment,
giddy and struggling
to find my center.

Midair, I question
whether
this thing, us
is merely
unbridled passion
or the deepest
of felt loves.

You always bring
me to the edge
of breathless.

Edge of Breathless

Waves of You

*You blend the warmth
of crimson sunsets
and ochre daybreaks,
coloring the span
between them
in deep layers
of a truthfulness
that cannot be escaped.*

*Now, I feel
in full color.
My life no longer
feels scripted or dulled.
The way you free me
is spiritual.*

You Free Me

Michelle G. Stradford

Your patience
was an
irresistible magnet
that drew me in.

You found little pathways
of connections
between us,
revealing your intention
a little each day,
building trust and desire,
pushing my doubts away
and lifting my
expectations higher.

When our lips finally met,
your love tasted
like a confession
of the sweetest
kind of confection.

Confession

Every magical moment
that I am with you,
I feel as if I have entered
a mysterious kingdom
lined with stardust.

When we rise
to dance and sing,
heartily celebrating life,
I am convinced we can
achieve anything,
because you make
me believe
that together we are
a perfect alchemy.

Enchanted

*Building a sacred
bond of trust,
we have propelled ourselves
into a wondrous place
that neither of us
has ever seen.
We have felt things
that we had never allowed
ourselves to believe.*

*We've been transported
into a world
with no need for armor
or shields.
We were moved,
finally free
to truly live openly
and love wholly.*

Moved

Waves of You

My fingertips are warmed
by your restless breath,
blowing kisses
as if you had never left.

Uncertain whether
it is genuinely you
or an apparition
walking
and strolling mystically
in the flesh,
right there beaming in
your own skin.

Yet still, you hold
my heart steady
and I'm forever your captive.
Our all-powerful love
is suspended
between today's realm
and the unknown.

My Mystic Love

Michelle G. Stradford

This foreign place
entangles me
in endless possibilities,
conflating last night's dream
with tomorrow's
stark reality.

A short flight
to my yesterday
threatens to dissipate
this raging passion
and returns us
to our sedated existences
before we flirted with fire
and danced in a fantasy.

Entangled

Your waves rush in
innocently caressing
my hand.
You tease at my shore
because you can.

Even though you profess
to genuinely care,
I watch warily
as your dangerous tide rises,
praying you'll carry
me with you
into your boundless sea.

Dangerous Tides

Michelle G. Stradford

*In each other's arms
we have finally found
a sanctuary
where our hearts
can beat unbounded,
keep one another warm,
and nurtured
in belonging.*

*We finally share
a beautiful home
custom-made
and filled with
enough love
for two hungry souls
to grow in.*

Shared Home

Waves of You

**Breezy images
replay in my mind
on an endless loop
of umbrella-lined
Carolina beaches.**

**We stroll on the baking sand,
with intertwined fingers
and clasped hands
humming beach tunes
as guitar strings strain
over the ocean roar.**

**We laugh at the seagulls
singing high
and swooping in
low and graceful
for a shady landing
in the Myrtle trees.
Then off they soar!**

Michelle G. Stradford

Our sun-drenched smiles
end the lazy day
with a longing
that stretches
for miles of shore.

We seal our promise
to rekindle this romance
after dinner with more
sugar tea kisses
in the peach twilight.

You are the sounds
of sanguine summers,
nostalgia and romance,
my vintage first love.

Sanguine Summer

Waves of You

You are clearly lying.
Why continue
with the false protests?
Please cease pretending
that you have
just now realized
your impact on me.

You are fully aware
that the inferno
fueling your eyes,
always brings on heat
higher than
I am equipped
to turn down.

Heated Lies

Michelle G. Stradford

I do not always hear
the words
you say to me,
because when your lips
are moving,
and your voice
is speaking,
my heart
starts swaying
to the love songs
you were always singing
while we strolled alone
on Litchfield beach
by the sea.

By the Sea

*I carried you across
perilous oceans
and tripped through
emotional minefields
just to gaze
into your eyes
while we bathed
in the rising heat vapors
of a thousand
summer suns.*

*All, so I could
bask in you.*

Basking

I study you through
filtered lenses,
cautious
but still drawn in
by the seductive sound
of your baritone,
made to simulate
intimate songs
only shared by two.

Your voice alters words
and makes me believe
that we communicate
in the same language
and covet a shared love.

Yet, we both know
we are reveling in
borrowed lies…

Borrowed Lies

Water flows for miles
as this ocean rises
and engulf us,
yet we cannot drown
this desire.

Nothing can put out
the fire
burning out of control
like a wayward sun
transforming the night
into endless days
of ecstasy and delight.

The Fire

Michelle G. Stradford

IMMERSED

When our two
hearts joined,
we became so much
more than one,
looming larger than
the stars, moon
and universe combined,
far brighter than
the blazing sun.

We created a union
so powerful
that it exploded
into a transformative
golden mist,
an elixir that erased
all things tragic
and fixed everything
that had held
us back
in this world.

Together, we made
a life that
brandished magic
like it was nothing.

Magic Life

Waves of You

You acknowledged
my recurring pain,
allowing me
the space and time
to heal again.

Then, you took
my hands in yours
day after day
and massaged my scars
until the hurt fell away.

You held onto me tightly
while we watched
my darkest demons
morph into the gray past,
finally, back
where they belong.

Held

Michelle G. Stradford

We repair our faults
with understanding,
dismiss our mistakes
with forgiveness,
and nurture one another
with compassion
so that our
imperfect love
continues to grow
and flourish.

Imperfect Love

Waves of You

Unreceptive to touch,
your somber silence
holds me prisoner.

I attempt to resuscitate
any feeling that remains,
then sense a faint throb,
halting breaths
and a rise in your chest.

My hope springs free,
holding your responsiveness
as evidence
that a dormant flame glows
beneath your reticence.

I am here for you, for us.
Depression will never
defeat us.

Reticence

Michelle G. Stradford

I pray that each instance
you recall
our time on the shore,
the weightiness of our love
and the heartlines
we drew in the sand
will inspire you to keep going,
until you make it home
to me once more.

Lines Drawn

We rejoice in belonging,
knowing that,
in each other,
we have finally found
a love that runs deep
and fills us with hope.

Our bond is strengthened
in the understanding
that our refusal
to give up on us
in the face
of life's toughest
challenges
has made our happy
perpetual.

Perpetual

Despite how hard I try,
I cannot find
the genesis of our bliss.

There does not appear
to be a beginning to us;
no first moment
when our "we" began.

All that matters
is that we just exist
in this here and now
and our love
has no bottom or end.

Blissful

As long as we treat
other people's opinions
of us as poisonous,
we will remain
insulated and inoculated
against distractions
and harmful influences.

Putting you and me
above all else,
raising our love up
and building a forever home
in the hearts of each other
makes us into
an unbreachable fortress.

Fortress

*The credits are scrolling
and the story is ending,
but this epic love
is just beginning.
Our curtains will
not be closing
just yet...*

Epic Beginning

Waves of You

I fell for the same you,
that exacting smile
and those sarcastic quips
years ago.

You challenged me then
to go toe-to-toe
as much as the person
standing right here
does today.

Yes, I am loving
your same
nerdy swagger
and hearty laughter
now more than
ever before.

Same You

*I know that you
are expecting
me to leave,
but I will keep creating
reasons for you
to believe
in me, in us
and show you
that our love
has changed me
in ways
I need you to see.*

Changed Me

We scarcely catch
each other's eyes
and rarely sense
a quickened pulse
or the thrill
from an accidental brush
of bared skin
the way we once did.

The trappings of life
threatens to drain
our happy away
so, I am
recommitting today
to make you
and our relationship
my number one priority.

Top Priority

Michelle G. Stradford

With you, I never
need to explain
what drives me,
or slow my stride
so, you can keep pace.

You do not expect
me to reign in
my self-pride,
dumb myself down
or apologize
for what I am not.

You intuitively feel
what I see,
and never attempt
to constrain me.

Waves of You

When I say
that someday
I will touch the sky,
you urge me
to break free
and stretch wide
to reach it now.

You lift me
even higher
than my mind's eye
can see.

You Break Me Free

**Keep your heart
dialed up to warm
so that the love
you set free
knows it will be
welcomed home,
judgment-free
when it returns,
holding back tears
and disillusioned,
after roaming for years
from one cold arm
to another.**

Warmed Hearts

Waves of You

I need you more each day
as you eagerly celebrate
my womanly virtues,
largesse attitudes and strength.
You meet me where I am,
while encouraging
me not to let up
on my breakthrough.

I trust you because
you intuitively understand
how my journey and history
have shaped me.
You never once
attempted to belittle,
or diminish.

I honor you because
you are strong enough
not to perceive
my perpetual motion
and need for control
as a threat
to the security
of your manhood.

I love you because
you accept me
for whom I am,
yet inspire me
to become all that I can.
You love me without
restraint with a heart
that knows no limit
and a mind filled
with virtues.

Virtuous

Even though I am uncertain
of the exact attraction
that brought you to me,
we have the perfect mix
of lasting allure.

After all these years,
you still excite me.
Our sparks never fail
to engage and ignite.

Lasting Allure

Thank you for being
strong enough
for both of us,
even when you feel
weaker than
the storm-torn trees
braving gale-force winds
that no one else sees.

Yet still, you carry
with stoic grace
all that has brought us
to our knees.
You lift those burdens
that are much
too heavy for me.

Stoic Grace

We must find a way
to ignore any
lingering questions,
and shut out any
unfounded doubts.

Focusing only on us
will lead the way
out of this maze,
helping us outdistance
the past,
and walk on the path
to a future that lasts.

Advancing

Michelle G. Stradford

You catch my eyes
to exchange a smile
and insist we slow down
for a while
to enjoy the little things.

With an outstretched hand,
you gently lift my chin
and a sudden rush
of sparks ignite again,
swirling and lighting
the way back to when
I first got caught up
in your brown-eye gaze,
and that mischievous grin.

Our memories return us
to the place where
we fell hard
and were completely smitten,
determined and committed
to forever protecting
this rarest of love.

These nostalgic trips
are always healing
and purely magical.
Promise me you will
invite me along again?

Nostalgic Trips

I am determined
to keep us on
the same page
and not allow you
to look away.

I pray that my words
served up naked,
revealing my vulnerability
will compel a reaction,
and make you feel
something,
before you close
the book on us.

Naked Words

The challenges
we have faced
and rapids
we have ridden,
have humbled
and strengthened us.

They have
revealed hidden
lessons that an
easy life
rarely teaches.

We have learned
just how deep
this powerful river
that is our love
reaches.

Love Reaches

*Even in the face
of bad days, besieged
by dark challenges
and mired in frustration,
we resist slipping
into sullen dismay.*

*We yield to the wind,
holding each other up.
Our union
may be challenged,
but we still stand,
committed
to building
us stronger.*

Stronger Us

Michelle G. Stradford

Our love is no longer
new and eager to please,
running fast, freely giving
way past its prime
and my skin has loosened
from my once-chiseled chin.

These bright eyes
used to shine for you,
but are now lined with years
of circles that reflect
the life we share.

Will you still reach
for me and play melodies
on my heartstrings
or sing me sweet promises
when we grow old?
Whisper to me again
that our twosome
will never part
and this love
shall never end.

Heartstrings

*As we celebrate
the birth of our love,
we commit all over again
to growing
and evolving it
into an everlasting garden
that keeps
our hearts singing
and hopes springing
eternally.*

Our Anniversary

Michelle G. Stradford

You took a chance
and treasured our union,
never giving up on us
through the heartaches,
all the joys and tears.

You have shown me
the meaning of trust,
immortalizing our love
through these
earthbound years
and beyond in an
an everlasting flame.

Immortal Love

Your love is
my yellow umbrella,
towering above all others
as the rain pours,
bright and hopeful,
deflecting life's storms,
sheltering over me
and covering us.

My Cover

Loving you is not
a weakness
that brings me
to my knees;
it gives me strength,
lifting me beyond
false horizons.

You help me see
far beyond myself
for a glimpse
into our infinity.

Horizons

*No, I cannot end
your waves of pain,
but I will lift you up
and always
raise you higher,
so, you can rise
above them.*

Lift You

Michelle G. Stradford

**Our love continues
to bloom in silence
through the stillness
of night,
growing our hearts
stronger
and entangling
our roots.**

**It searches our souls
for sustenance,
while our hands
tightly clasp together
in the protection
of restorative sleep.**

Bloom in Silence

*I have little use
for your past
and no patience
for any of my doubts.*

*My interest only lies
in the things
I can trust
and believe in today.*

*Our unwavering faith
manifests a future
that already
belongs to us.*

Unwavering Faith

I do not seek
solutions
or expect ready answers.
I am not looking
for you to save me.
I only need your open
and protective heart
to listen intently,
really hear
and understand
my thoughts.

What I want
from you
is to feel your arms
enfolding me
in comfort and for you
to hold my hand
so, I never
get lost
in my dark
hiding places.

What I Want

*Commitment
is not allowing
each other
to turn away
from the messy side
of love.
It defines the meaning
of an Us.*

Commitment

I sat in silence
while you traveled
deep to retrieve
your peace.

I have been
to your edge,
and seen
the rivers raging
inside of you.

I did not run away,
and will never
leave you to ride
the dangerous
rapids alone.

Rivers Raging

The new sheen
from
original love
is long gone
and filmed over.
We covered it in layers
of anniversaries,
afterschool schedules,
global work trips,
finger-painted faces,
puppies and chores.

Though badly tarnished
and gone unpolished
for years,
I can still catch a glint
of joy in our union.
Lying beneath
the wear and tear
of the dog-eared pages
of our lives
are happy faces.

I hear loud laughter dancing
as I hover over faded
family photographs
where we can see
our complicated
happily ever after
still gleaming.

Our Happily Ever After

Through the years
of unintended neglect,
the strength of our love
always knew how
to find the sunlight.

It pushed through
our cracks and grew
around the edges,
filling in the gaps
making us stronger.

Love Knows

*I am not here
to attempt to fix
or rescue you.
I fell for your
flaws first
because you
trusted in us
enough
to show me
your raw truth.*

Raw Truth

Your eyes will forever
be my compass,
leading my heart
to wherever you travel.

I lose direction
when I cannot see
the warmth and hope
in your smile
beaming at me
and lighting our way home
for years and miles
to come.

Light Beams

Waves of You

My mind sifts through
a year of ordinary
images and memories
of us, of you.
They filled in holes,
and shut down the doubts
that kept closing doors.

My jaded heart believes
in the impossible
once more.
Our dreams for a future
are now renewed.

Life is extraordinary,
made shiny and new
with every magical day
I spend in
the presence of you.

Year to Renew

*I promise to shield
your flame
from the ravages
of life's relentless winds.*

*Whatever it takes,
I will keep lighting
your candles
over and over again.*

Eternal Flame

Waves of You

Your outstretched hand
led me back
to our brief summer
by the fountain
where love was
springing free,
as falling for you
came so easily
and as inevitable
as the fog eclipsing
the Blue Ridge peaks.

Back then,
all I could see
was the eventuality
of our lips
colliding and exploding
into a future
of replicas of you
and miniature me's.

Yes, just as it was always
intended to be...

Futures Spring

Michelle G. Stradford

**The way your eyes
instantaneously
dance in lights
when you look at me
just as they did
the day you rolled back
my clouds,
makes me believe
that I *am* the sunlight.**

The Sunlight

At the sight of you,
I frantically search
for my shut-off valve
to save myself
from being carried away
by floods of emotion
amid the memories
that overtake me.

Then, suddenly
I am rising again,
trying to ride
these waves of you
that have never
stopped surging.

Waves of You

Michelle G. Stradford

From the Author

I am grateful you completed reading *"Healing Grace."* I hope you found comfort, affinity, and inspiration in the poetry and prose.

Feedback, whether a phrase, a brief sentence or a paragraph, is valued and appreciated. Your input helps me validate my themes and informs me about what I should write next. So, please take a moment to leave a rating and review online at the retailer site where you purchased this book.

To stay updated on my next book release, read samples of work in progress, etc., please connect with me:

TikTok @michellestradford
Instagram @michellestradfordauthor
Twitter @mgstradford
Facebook @michellestradfordauthor
Pinterest @michellestradfordauthor
Bookbub: michelle-g-stradford
Goodreads: Michelle G Stradford

 Subscribe to my newsletter for book release updates, promotions, and giveaways by scanning code or search https://linktr.ee/michellestradford

Acknowledgments

As I was writing my latest romantic poetry collection, I was reminded of the unique experiences along my journey to finding my soulmate.

For much of this book, my husband was my source of inspiration. He wrote and sang an original song as his proposal and has since serenaded me through the good and the challenging moments in life. I thank him for his support and patience, especially when writing becomes all-consuming as I focus my intensity on meeting a deadline.

I also owe my appreciation to my daughters, who listen with patience as I wax on about the writing process, book covers, etc. They continue to be my inspiration.

Thank you to my editor Eva Xan for pushing me to refine my words and sharpen my messages to create my readers' best experience.

And finally, thank you to the readers who continue to purchase and read my books. Those of you who reach out to share how my words have encouraged you or helped others keeps me going. I am grateful to each of you.

EXCERPTS FROM SELF LOVE COLLECTION

Self Love Notes: Uplifting Poetry, Affirmations & Quotes

Someday I will grow
brave enough
to carefully unfurl my secrets
and watch them free-fall
in velvet blankets,
like the petals of a rose
finally discovering
the beauty of freedom
now that they
are no longer trapped
inside the folds
of my soul.

My Secrets

Self Love Notes II: Affirming Poetry & Prose

You are far stronger
than you have imagined.
Never underestimate
your capacity to battle
your fiercest enemy
then soar high
despite the damage
sustained by your wings.

Soar Steadily

SCAN QR CODE TO GET A SIGNED COPY OF BOOK

About the Author

Michelle G. Stradford is a bestselling Author, Architect, Artist, and Photographer who creates written, visual, and inhabitable art. Besides poetry, she has written short stories and fiction since adolescence. Her writing style is contemporary free verse, as her goal is to create poetry and prose that is relatable, connects with, and is inspiring to her readers.

In particular, she wants to use her experiences and writing to build a platform that encourages women and girls to own their power to overcome challenges and crush their goals. Michelle is married and has two daughters.

EXCERPTS FROM ROMANTIC COLLECTION

Waves of You: Love Poems

Your love does not
take my breath away.
It breathes life into me,
no matter how high
you lift my soul
or how deep
you send me
searching.

Soul Search

When Love Rises

I inhaled the breath
you exhaled
and in a singular moment
we breathed life
into this
extraordinary love.

Kissed to Life

SCAN QR CODE TO GET A SIGNED COPY OF BOOK

Other Books

by Michelle G. Stradford

Inspirational Poetry

I'm Rising: Determined. Confident. Powerful.

Rise Unstoppable

Healing Grace: Inspirational Poetry for Coping & Closure

Self Love Notes II: Affirming Poetry & Prose

Self Love Notes: Uplifting Poetry, Affirmations & Quotes

Romantic Love Poetry

Waves of You: Love Poems

When Love Rises

Michelle G. Stradford

www.ingramcontent.com/pod-product-compliance
Lightning Source LLC
Chambersburg PA
CBHW030000110526
44587CB00011BA/921